mania

Jeffrey-Paul Horn

Clare Songbirds Publishing House Chapbook Series
ISBN 978-1-947653-04-7
Clare Songbirds Publishing House
Mania © 2107 Jeffrey-Paul Horn
All Rights Reserved. Clare Songbirds Publishing House retains right to reprint.
Permission to reprint individual poems must be obtained from the author who owns the copyright.

Printed in the United States of America
FIRST EDITION

Clare Songbirds Publishing House Mission Statement:
Clare Songbirds Publishing House was established to provide a print forum for the creation of limited edition, fine art from poets and writers, both established and emerging. We strive to reignite and continue a tradition of quality, accessible literary arts to the national and international community of writers, and readers. We support our literary artists with high quality services and on-going support. Chapbook manuscripts and art quality poetry broadsides are carefully chosen for their ability to propel the expansion of art and ideas in literary form. We provide an accessible way to promote the art of words in order to resonate with, and impact, readers not yet familiar with the siren song of poets and writers. Clare Songbirds Publishing House espouses a singular cultural development where poetry creates community and becomes commonplace in public places.

Clare Songbirds Publishing House
140 Cottage Street
Auburn, New York 13021

Contents

Wicked Laura Lee	5
Lost by Your Window	6
Sometimes	7
Scar Tissue	8
Sex Poem	10
Emptiness	11
While I ache…	12
The Transient Prophet	13
My Labyrinth	14
Loneliness	15
The Scream	17
Stuck	18
Another	19
Mastodon in Mittens	21
Lost in silence…	22
I	23
Texas breakfast	24
Guardian	26

The Transient Prophet initially published in *aaduna*, Volume 7, No. 2

Mastodon modified by L.W. French from James St. John's *Reconstruction of Mammut americanum*

Wicked Laura Lee

A wee little way into the passage way
lies a majestic mystic fireball

A hired man's hand in the promise land
ready and waiting to take the fall

Creep with me to wicked Laura Lee
and weep at the final phony's plight
Take what you must before the big bust
and fade away gracefully in the night

some say it seems like a foolish man's dream
to get past our hand made frustrations
But all we need here along with bourbon and beer
is a touch of natural man's patience

Lost by Your Window

Stay lost by your window
waiting for air

Stay lost by your window
but he never cared

Heart throb caribou
get lost in my winds
Sex scenes, infidelity
remember these sins

Love and loss, then the great rouse
Stay loving life's mysteries
and searching for clues

Sometimes

Sometimes I sit and think
What if I forever sit and think

to escape the disappointment
and touch the fire of the sun

I'd rewind to my beginnings
and take a wayward trail

shun the earth as a whole
not become what I've become

My songs would be lullabies
carols of an enlightened heart

in big and full beginnings
my survival would be an art

Love's script awaiting edit
remaining on the shelves

until we see the shining light
and learn to be ourselves

A new moon would beckon
under which we'd tell our story

at the reception of affection
and everlasting glory

Scar Tissue

You're just scar tissue
another issue

it leaves me hurt
and fucking pissed too

Drunk again I loom

In the lowdown towns
where clowns come to drown
their painted on frowns
and die

I wonder why

Why our fantasies must be fallacies
Why I'd be glad to see you mad at me
'cause at least then I'd know you thought of me

But you don't

I knew you'd come to me

But you won't

In my manic madness landscape
your city sadness resonates

I still have to live here you know

These flowers withered
These fucking dreams

I'm a sidewalk slave

Birth-Pain- Grave

Sex Poem

In spite of you
I am
inside of you

Emptiness

All the rooms have wolves inside
mind's eye blue

The men roam aimlessly
biding their time until the end

The women laugh
lusting their losses
carrying the burdens of insanity

Nothing is real here
nothing is earned

Were nothing but soul-less cadavers
waiting

So come children
time to feast on the weak
time to follow the herd
to the edge of nowhere
-emptiness

While I ache to be free

Society looms
unleashing it's doom
upon me

I'm frightened

A cold scared pawn of greater forces

I'm hungry
I'm weak

I'm used up
My energy given to those who bind me

Lost
while still in the clutch of the master

How am I free when chained?
How am I rich when destitute?
How am I fed and still hungry?

Still bound to the forces that feed upon me

The Transient Prophet

The transient prophet spoke only in poems

Dark denim destiny

He had lived in waves of amber
and forged long forgotten roads

Magic maidens cared for him
among throngs of shell shocked pawns

Morning mayhem warriors walk scarred
and anguished amidst the tortured fragments of civilization

Everyone here is lost

Just hopeless heaps
begging for answers

Yet nobody listened when the prophet spoke
Nobody heard a word

My Labyrinth

I live in a labyrinth
amongst the whispering hollows

They call my name
again and again

Do you not hear
at night in the clear
as the light of the moon
sets upon you

Strange vibrations
alive in the air

I drank a magic potion
and traded my mind for the truth

I am a man of fire and rage
a man so old while still in his youth

Loneliness

Loneliness defines me
I'm swept into waves of melancholy
Fear holds me from truth

I doubt my existence
as I fight my own saviors

A fire burns unquenched
by the passionless armadas of imbecilic slaves
that surround me
I surrender

Take me not fighting against your brutal foolery
Into my own diminutive hell

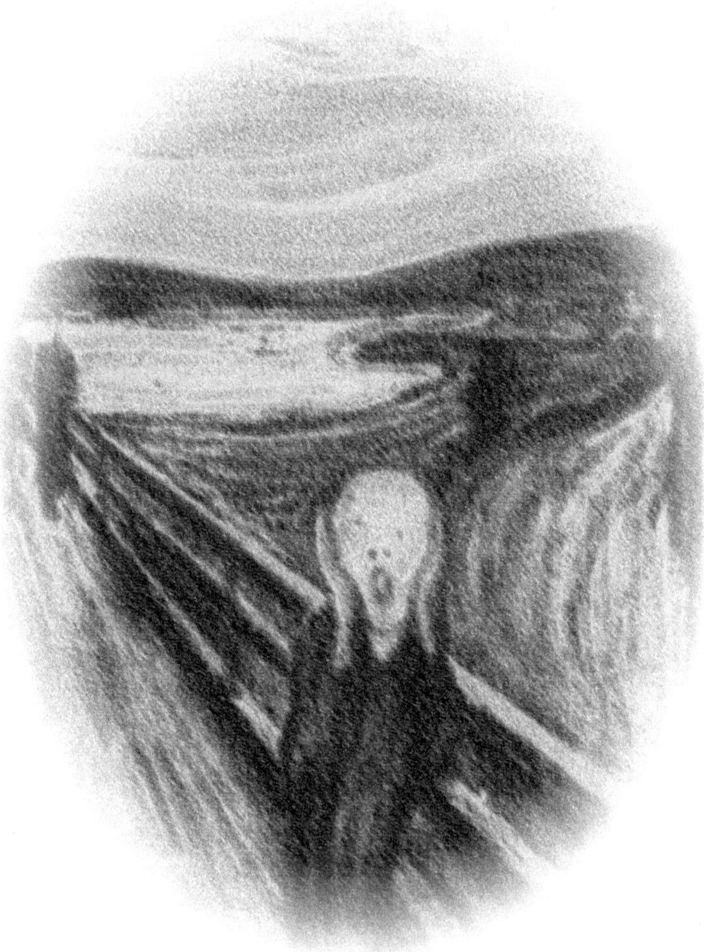

16

The Scream
inspired by the painting by Edward Munch

In the warm dew morning's dawn
a bastion of love

Sunshine horizons
surround my weary shell

The day grows warmer
contrary to my soul

Frustration, confusion, undying vulnerability
I've tried in vain to contain my madness

In a sea of swarming emotions
I am drowning

No longer can I fight
No longer can I hide

A burning buildup
with raging torment
I inhale

I start a reassuring word
but all I can muster

is the scream

Stuck

Soft contours slowly weather to sharp cracks

Why must time change me?

I......both nymph and nympho

both man and boy

-stuck

never quenched by life's nectar- I wallow

just a denizen of mire

From lonely road to lonely road
I am the dust

Tripping on life's poisons

a lush lost in a growing haze

This is the soliloquy of a shadow
a prophet lost to himself

a midnight maniac

a free man- still searching for an escape

still clinging to the chains that bind me

Another

Another bottle to ease the unheard voices
Another night alone
Another whisper from a long lost liar
assuring my demise will come
easy..........mercifully
There is only lust in the eyes of another lover
only hours in the grips of another night
Fancy free irreverence to stifle my untold truths

Mastodon

Mastodon in Mittens

I am a mastodon in mittens
A mutt bastard

I am a plasma fueled fledgling ape

I will rise early in the dawn of a new time to rule
your groveling masses

Soon the coming of a new energy will lead to an
ever expanding compendium of grace
that will shine upon me in an orgiastic mind fuck

Freak show horizons whip in frenzy before me
holding unknown cadavers to unknown oaths

In the permanent vastness
I wrestle with my impermanence
- asking for nothing more than
Escape

And I swallow my memories in vain moments of
bullshit camaraderie

Knowing that never means nothing and forever is
fallacy

We have forgotten the forgotten

Lost in silence
inevitable dismay

I play the hand that's dealt me

A reticent light
refusing to show itself

Some love dies in blue

True love lives in agony

I

I am quantum vastness
Consummate illusion
Here is nowhere
I am an ailing beast of self destruction
I am a helpless searcher

Texas Breakfast

Texas breakfast in the teeth of confusion
A wild wind of passion striding over me with each light
Rising winds washing my destiny in linen minefields
of my own tempestuous misogyny

Another fabled mystery in the patterns of mania

I am a moonstruck wanderer
a lover of your sins and a gentle reciprocator of your gifts

Nothing more than a symbol of love and the actualization
of young lust

I am a lost prophet
You are an angel led astray

We dance in a cosmic playground dressed as life

Astral explorers deep in love' plastic majesties

This labyrinth of mayhem
in this moment of doom

We dance on the teetering brink of reality

and you cum with me in deep agape of surrender

in longing light of full moon splendor

in dwindling days of full exuberance

You come with me into night

and I cherish you in morning

Guardian

There is a man
with bone through nose

sword and knife
arrows and bows

skeleton face
of bone and blood

a man of terror
war paint and mud

straw haired priest
he's donning skulls

surrounded by kinsmen
he strikes fear in all

Whether on high
in love or hate

I have a man
with ancient traits

with fiery aura
hellish frenzy

he beats a rhythm
never ending

on drum of skin
of vanquished foe
he beats his rhythm
wherever I go

Only once have I seen him
through wild haze

I knew he had been there
through all of my days

At morning sun
or in nights embrace

I feel his presence
in any space

In dawn of treachery
in times of low

there's a man behind me
this I know

Jeffrey-Paul Horn

Jeffrey-Paul Horn was born in Utica NY, but was raised in tiny Rome NY. He briefly attended the Art Institute of Pittsburgh.

Shortly after leaving school, he began writing music. Jeffrey began writing poetry as a boy, but became passionate about his content and craft as an adolescent. He has always retained an adventurous and rebellious spirit and wishes to pursue an alternative, agrarian lifestyle.

Currently Jeffrey resides in Syracuse NY, but has traveled extensively and lived in Tempe, Austin, Houston and St. Petersburg Florida.

www.ingramcontent.com/pod-product-compliance
Lightning Source LLC
Chambersburg PA
CBHW052130110526
44592CB00013B/1824